Marisa Wohlschlaeger

Marisa Wohlschlaeger

LOUD & QUEER

QUEER VOICES

OF NOW

QUEER LUNAR NEW YEAR

 Marisa Wohlschlaeger

QUEER LUNAR NEW YEAR

The new year can be a time of remembrance and a time of growth. For those that celebrate lunar new year, it can be a time when culture and family come up against identity and self. What does this time of year mean to you?

Because this zine contains the phases of life, like the light and dark side of the moon, the zine includes some content that isn't suitable for everyone. Please note the content warnings in the table of contents and at the top of each page.

Thank you for being a part of the LOUD & QUEER community. your interest and support is what allows us to create this zine and share queer voices of now.

BECOME A PATRON OF LOUD & QUEER ZINE AT **PATREON.COM/LOUDANDQUEERZINE**

CONTENTS

Content Warning Legend

[1] Violence   [2] Suicide   [3] Explicit Language

[4] Nudity   [5] Drugs

Zen & the Art of Swimming

By Rob McCabe

Water feels so sensuous
as it caresses my body,
like fine silk
or the hands of a lover.
I push gently through
seeing the ripples moving forward
like a ship coursing through the sea.
Back & forth,
back & forth,
my mind attuned
to the repetition--
A state of Zen.

Taking a breather in the shallow end,
leaning against the wall,
I watch the endless bodies
of swimmer-muscled Adonises
dive in the deep end,
piercing the water
like an arrow shot
from a Zen Master's bow.
Swimming underwater,
exhibiting muscular strength
like an amphibian
as they push through the deep,
controlling their breath for what seems
like an eternity.

As I begin my ritual of laps,
I look to my left,
then to my right,
fantasizing these swimmers
are naked, penetrating my body
as easily as they push through the water.

Following my workout,
which is more fun, than work,

I run to the showers
to avoid being seen by others,
as I struggle to prevent anyone
from seeing my arrow
pushing through my swimmer's trunks.
I shower, dry off, and leave,
while the swimmers
continue their ongoing rituals
of sport, mastering the element of water
& seduction of those of us
who can only dream of ecstatic kisses
And hot embraces.

Ecstasy

By Rob McCabe

A Golden Shovel poem,
based on Emily Dickinson's, "Wild Nights."

Oh God baby, how you drive me wild
The way we make love, all through our nights
Thunder crashing, lightning flashing, wild
Quiet days--vivid, passionate nights.
How I wish that you always were
Laying beside me and I
Could always be at peace with
You. Oh great Aphrodite, I sing my prayers to Thee
Oh babe, your kisses drive me wild
Through all of our blissful days and nights.
If I could be faithful to you, would
You be faithful to me? How would it be
Living our lives together, our
Passionate love making would be our luxury.

Growth

By Rob McCabe

Together, we grow towards tenderness,
With gentle words and soft, purrs,
Together, we grow towards the light.
Together, we grow through a gentle caress,
Across my lips, face, back, and thighs,
Even with a gentle bite,
Making love throughout the **night**.

Together, we grow towards each other.
Like moths to a candle's bright flame.
Together, we grow through the darkness,
Until the break of day.

Together, we grow through moans of pleasure,
Together, through tears of pain.
Together, we sing the body electric,
As true love begins again.

Together, we dream through the twilight,
That doesn't rise or set,
Together we will always remember,
And never, not ever, forget.

Note from the artist:

My name is Rob McCabe and I am Queer poet living in Gulfport, Florida, a small artistic community. In the summer of 2016, I received my MFA in Creative Writing from the University of Tampa. My poetry collection, "Junky," was published in July 2018 by Dark Horse Florida Publishing LLC and is currently available on www.barnesandnoble.com and amazon.com.

Kiss

By Magda N-W

Though I could not
contain the moon
my lips bruising
at her touch

I hold her
for a little while
in her darkest
hopeful time

Though I would not
fight the ocean
for she is ever
stronger than I

I hold her
swells to low tide
until she is ready
to strike again

Note from the artist:

Magda is a writer, activist and trained biochemist. She loves folklore, pop-culture and the stuff in between. A born and bred Londoner, when she isn't writing she working to promote accessible sustainability or caring for her ever-growing collection of house plants.

Revive Aries I Am

By Aries I Am aka. Angelica Angeles

Artist who drew me, how they captured me,
and is this me now
Or would there be a new me?

Artist: Lexington Wolcraft
@themightylexloo

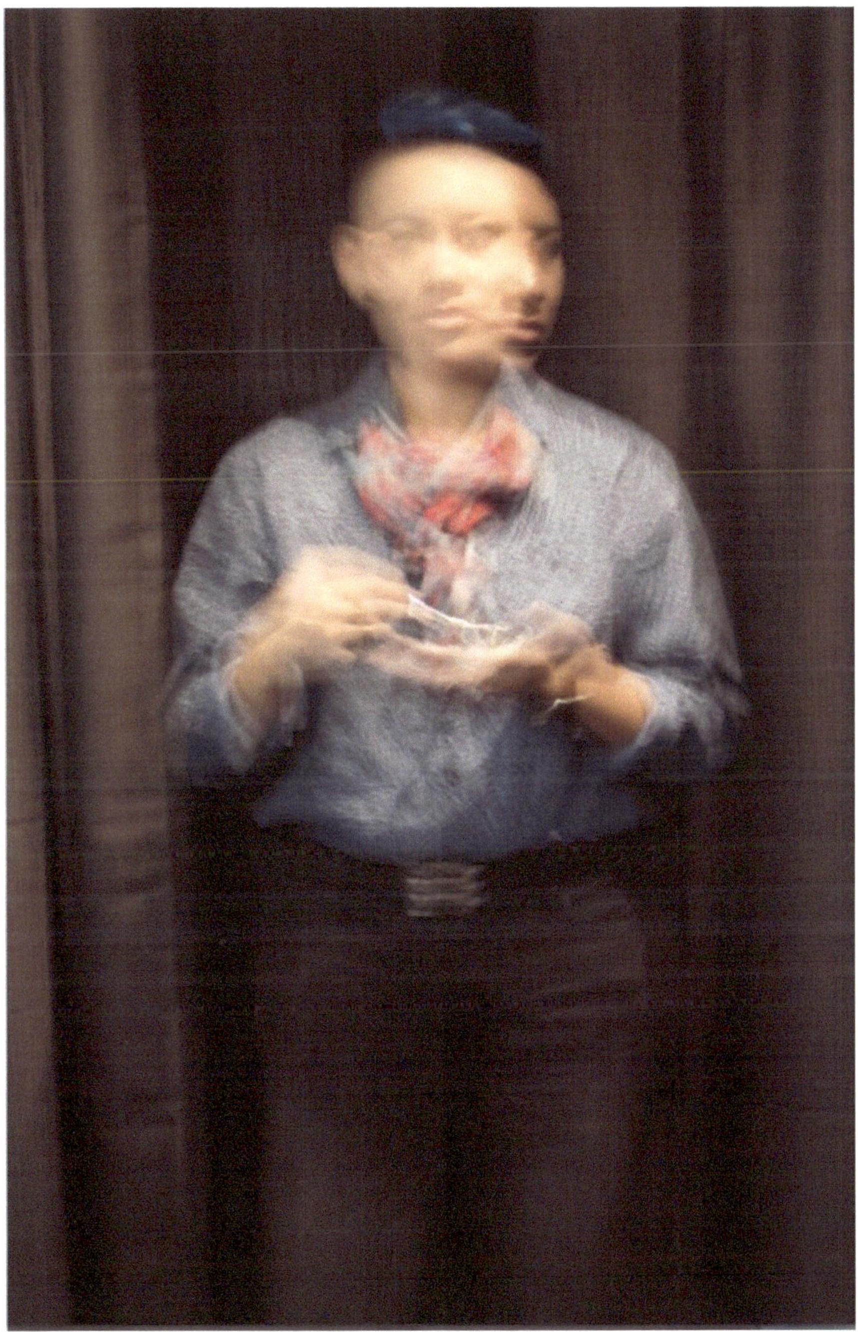

Artist: R Bear ChauDavis
@rbcdart

Artist: Jake Rose
@lookatjakerose

Lunar recharge me to reflect and find who I am at present.

Let me recharge them under my pillow during the "Full Moon".
-Angel

Dive
By Joseph Cavalieri

Note from the author:
I work with stained glass, design and production here in my studio in New York City. I focus on making one-of-a-kind commissions and art for exhibitions in the US and internationally. I specialize in contemporary stained glass, often based on fables and books.

Body Positivity

By Marisa Wohlschlaeger and Chris Mok

17

BECOME A PART OF OUR QUEER COMMUNITY

Our community of creators always needs new voices to add to the zine. Want to become a part of LOUD & QUEER?

Submit your writing, art, or other creations to:

loudandqueerzine@gmail.com

Please include 1) your name, 2) the name of your piece(s), and 3) 1-2 sentences to share with our readers.

We will consider your work for our next issue!

Share our call for submissions with LGBTQIA+ creators everywhere so we can give them a voice too!

THANK YOU to all the artists, writers, and creators who submitted their work and featured their pieces in LOUD & QUEER. The zine wouldn't be possible without you!

SUPPORT
LOUD & QUEER
NOW & FOREVER

LOUD & QUEER is committed to giving a voice to the queer community and projecting those perspectives into the wider community. We want everyone to hear queer voices of now, and that is why our zine is given out freely to all that want to read it.

We rely on patrons and donations to keep the zine going. Did you love this issue? Want new issues of LOUD & QUEER in the future? Want to receive exclusive perks and rewards while supporting LGBTQIA+ creators?

Become a patron of LOUD & QUEER
PATREON.COM/LOUDANDQUEERZINE

9 798360 510291